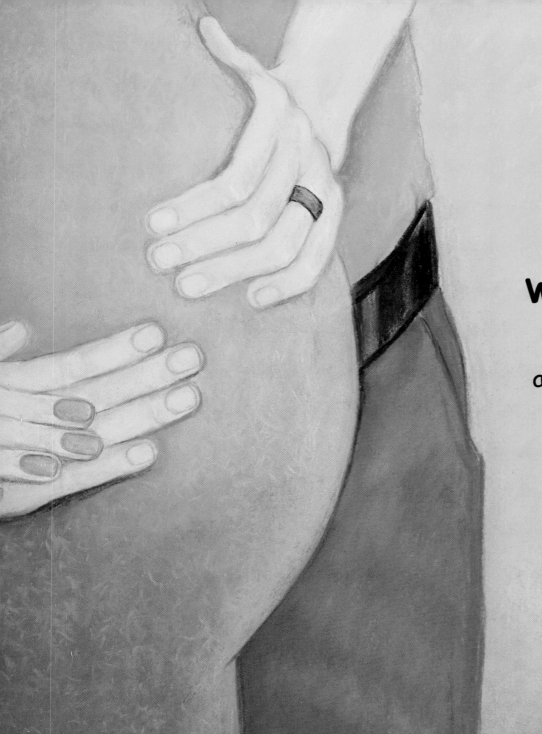

WoW! What a Trip!
was written to help
children feel wonderful
about being a big brother
or big sister.

For more information contact at: susan@wowwhatatripbook.com
Publication date: January 2018
ISBN Print: 978-0-9994314-0-5
ISBN eBook: 978-0-9994314-1-2
ISBN ePDF: 978-0-9994314-2-9

Library of Congress Control Number: 2017917358

This publication is designed to provide accurate and authoritative information in regard to the subject matter covered. It is sold with the understanding that the author or the publisher is not engaged in rendering any type of medical information. If expert assistance is required, the services of a competent medical professional should be sought.

1. Pregnancy 2. Baby 3. Conception 4. Embryo 5. Fetus 6. Sibling
I Tarrant, Susan. II WoW! What a Trip!: How to explain to your child a new baby is on the way.
WoW! What a Trip! may be purchased at special quantity discounts. Resale opportunities are available for sales promotions, hospitals, birthing centers, fundraising, book clubs, or educational purposes for churches, congregations, schools, and universities.

Have Susan speak at your organization or special event.
For information, call Susan at 941-216-0841 or email her susan@wowwhatatripbook.com
Illustrator: Susan Lavalley susanlavalleyillustr8r@gmail.com
Layout and Design: Shannon Tarrant
Photographer: Kathy Thomas, KathyThomas.com
Website: wowwhatatripbook.com
Publishing Consultant: Mel Cohen of Inspired Authors Press LLC inspiredauthorspress.com
Publisher: WoW Publishing
Printed in the United States of America

Dedication

WoW! What a Trip! is dedicated to my parents Mildred and John, my brother Larry, my husband Steven, his parents Miriam and Robert, and his sister Edith. I also thank the many angels that helped make this book possible.

Look, I'm me!

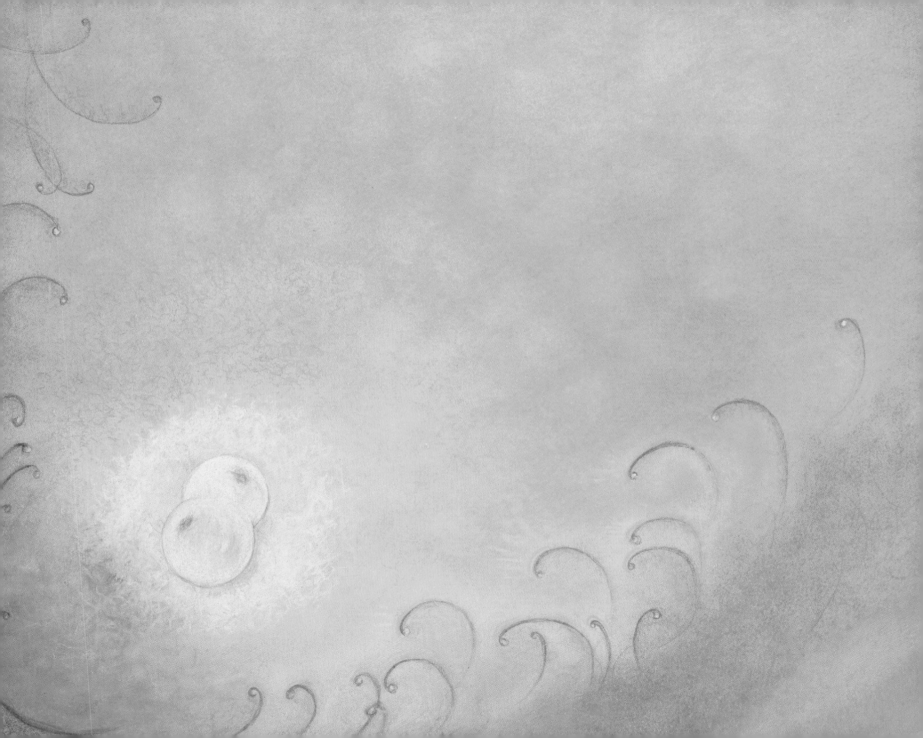

Hey! I just got bigger.

Look at that!
I'm connected to mommy.

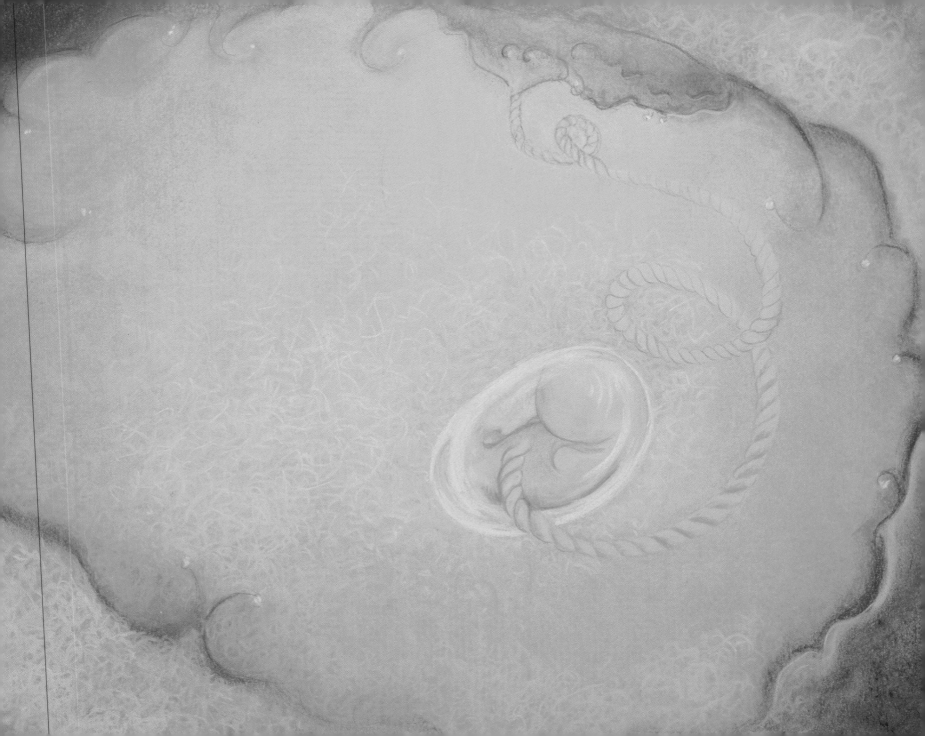

WoW!
I have arms and legs.

I hear lots of sounds.
I wonder what's a buddy.

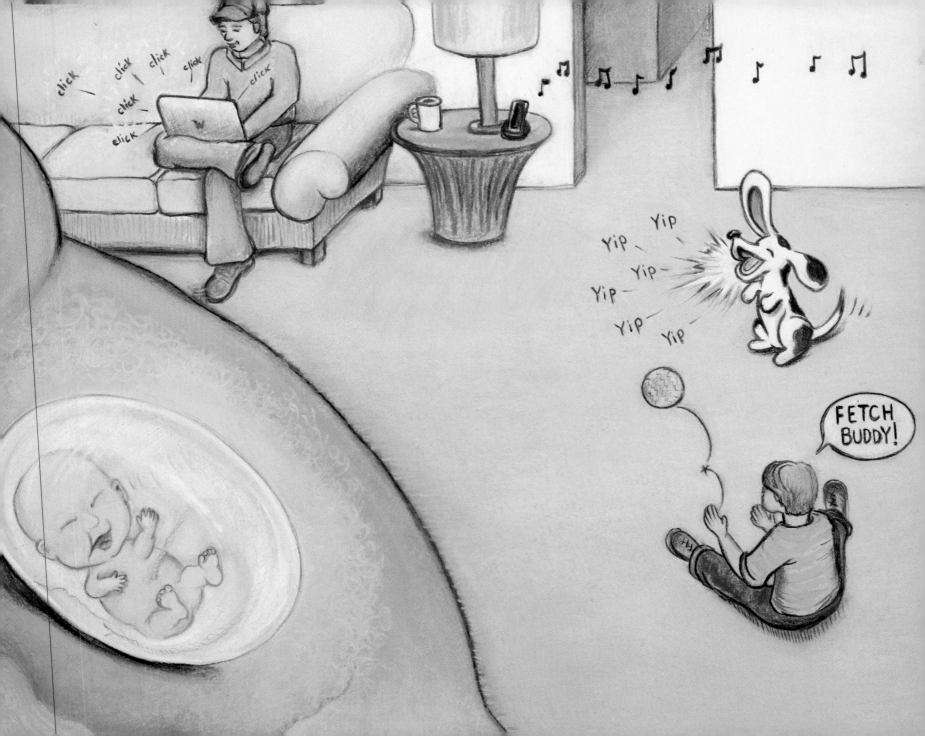

Oooo...Fingers and toes!
I wonder what they do.

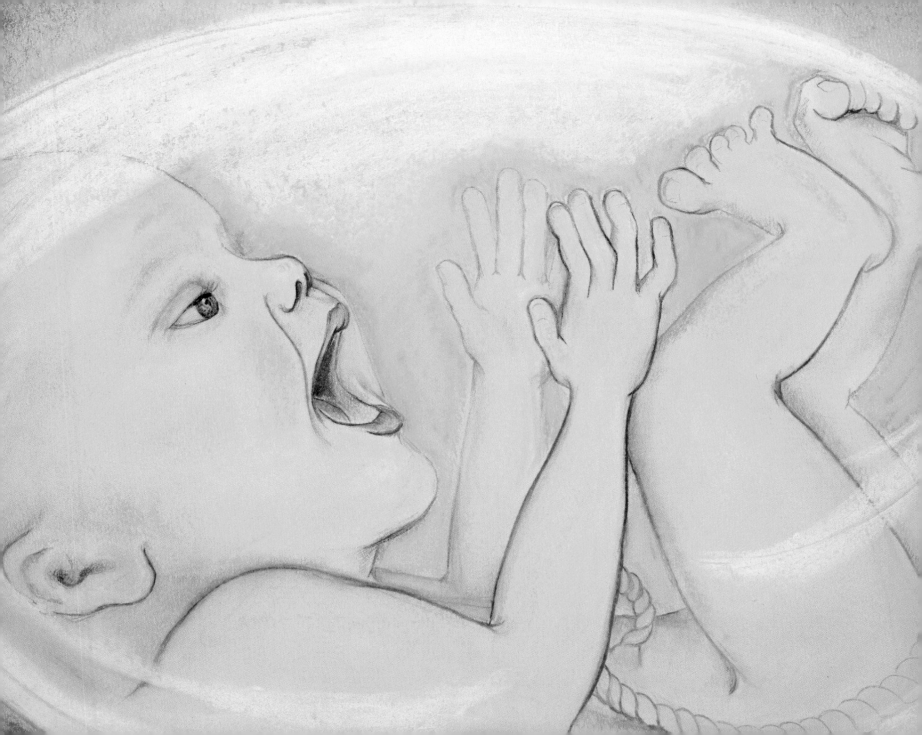

They're taking pictures of me.
I'll give them a big smile.

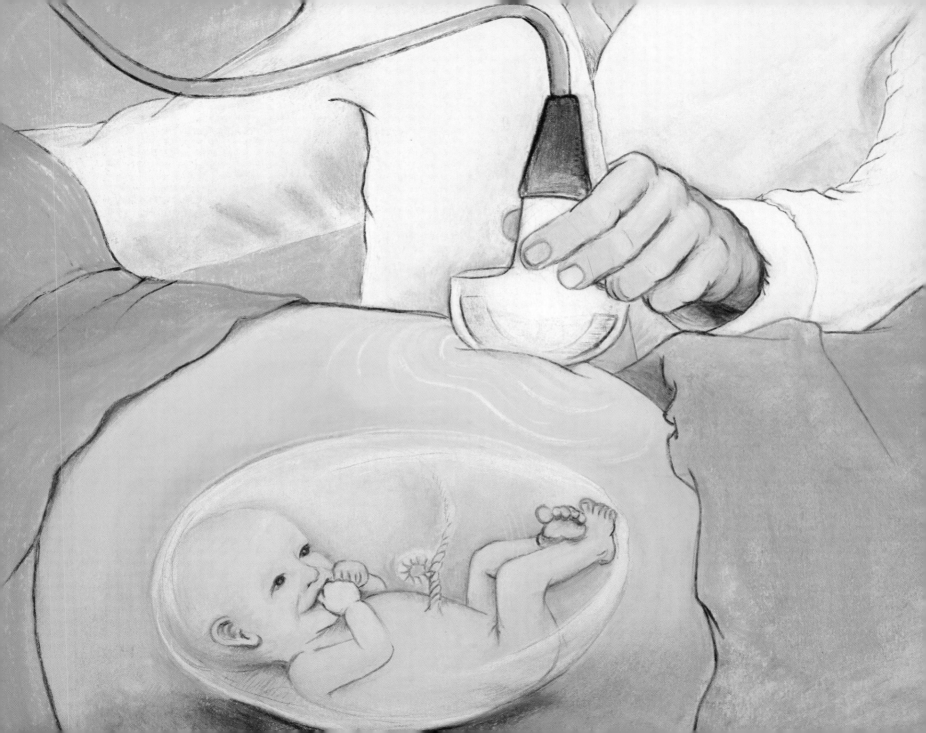

Oh no!
Pickles and ice cream again!

When I push on mommy's tummy,
I feel someone pushing back.
That's lots of fun!

I wonder what my name will be.

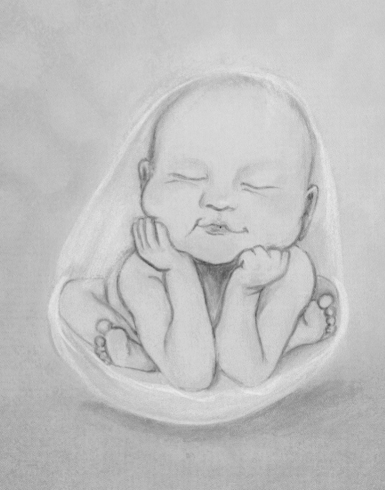

Will my family be ready for me?
I wonder if I'll have a
big brother or big sister.

I just heard,
"I can't wait to hold
our baby."

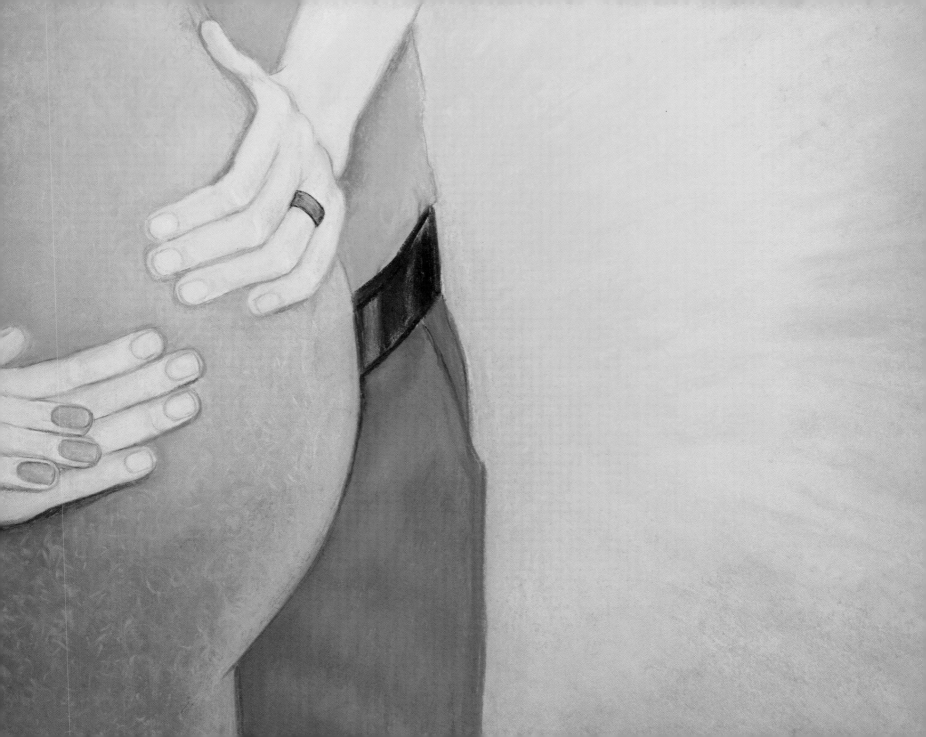

Wheee...
I'm going somewhere really fast.
Hey! Watch out for those bumps.

It's time to be with my family!

WoW!
What a Trip!
It's my birthday!

Family Photos

Family Photos

Memories

The date we discovered that we were pregnant:_____

Our reaction:_____

_____

_____

_____

Their reaction: _____

_____

_____

_____

Memories

Mom's Cravings:_____

_____

Our labor story:_____

_____

_____

_____

_____

Due Date:_____   Birthdate:_____

Time:_____   Hospital:_____

Weight:_____   Length:_____

How big I get on my journey

When I became me	I'm about the size of a grain of sugar.
About 8 weeks (2 months)	I'm the size of a jelly bean, peanut M&M or a small Lego brick.
About 12 weeks (3 months)	Now, I'm about the size of a toy soldier or a chicken nugget.
About 16 weeks (4 months)	I'm about the size of an action figure or a cell phone.
About 20 weeks (5 months)	I've grown to the size of a paper airplane or a tall glass of milk.
About 24 weeks (6 months)	A child's baseball mitt or a Barbie Doll. That's how big I am now.
About 28 weeks (7 months)	I'm as big as a Barbie convertible car or a lunch box.
About 32 weeks (8 months)	It looks like I'm about the size of a loaf of bread.
About 36 weeks (9 months)	Gee. I'm as big as tiny dog or a cabbage patch doll.
About 40 weeks	Look at that. I'm the same size as small beach ball or a small watermelon.

For the Parents

WoW! What a Trip! was written to help explain to your child that a new baby is on the way. The goal of the illustrations is to create and develop conversations with your child. The easiest way to do this is by asking questions.

The pictures in this book will provide many talking points about what happens during the stages of pregnancy. The goal is to help your child or children understand that the pregnancy is truly all about love.

Suggestions for discussion with your child

Look, I'm me! A great way to open this conversation is to say, "Mommy and Daddy love each other so much and because we love you so much, we have decided to have a new baby. Right now, our new baby is growing in a special place in mommy's tummy."

Hey! I just got bigger. Here you might want to say something like "In that special place in mommy's tummy, the little cells keep making more and more cells that will soon look like our baby." You could also add, "all the cells that are growing will make a little boy or little girl." Then share how happy you would be with either one."

I hear lots of sounds. I wonder what's a buddy? Our baby really likes hearing all different noises like us talking or laughing or listening to music. Sometimes the baby can even hear a dog barking or fireworks popping. You can tell the baby that you love him/her very much and can't wait to see them. Would you like to say something to our baby?

Suggestions Continued

They're taking pictures of me. I'll give them a big smile. Mommy has to go to the doctor for regular checkups. Sometimes the doctor uses a special camera so we can see our new baby growing. If you have an ultrasound picture, you could say "Sometimes the doctor even takes a picture of our baby. Would you like to see it?"

Oh No! Pickles and ice cream again! You could say, "Look at the baby's face in the picture. Do you think the baby is happy? I think that sometimes I might eat things that maybe our baby doesn't like. Sometimes you might think that what I am eating isn't very good either."

I just heard "I can't wait to hold our baby." You might ask your child or children "Do you think you will like holding our baby?" You could also let them know that sometimes babies get a stinky diaper when you are holding them. You can just let us know if that happens (be sure to laugh if you use this suggestion).

*Download the **FREE** complete Parent Guide with more questions to ask your child and conversation ideas. Find the guide at **wowwhatatripbook.com**.*

About the Illustrator

Susan Lavalley is from Lake Placid, NY, a tiny Olympic Village in the Adirondack Mountains. Susan's love of illustration was developed at the Cleveland Institute of Art where she also refined talents in the traditional craft of Metalsmithing and Classic Enamelwork. Years later, Susan joined the SCBWI, Society of Children's Book Writers and Illustrators, where she then discovered a purity of communication with children through drawing. Her professional experience includes a personally illustrated and authored children's book "Humble Heart" and also "Green Frog Village" commissioned by published author Tim Hammer Johnson. She currently resides on the Gulf Coast in St. Petersburg, Florida with her husband Pete Weaver. Susan is an accomplished Master Oil Painter and Pastelist. Her artwork can be seen online at SusanLavalley.com.

About the Author

Susan M. Tarrant is a long time resident of Bradenton, FL, but lived most of her life in the Northeast. She was educated at Eastern Michigan University in Special Education and taught special needs children for many years. She has been a small business owner, a recruiter and a career counselor. Her most important job, however, has been that of mother and grandmother. Family means everything to her! Her retirement and the love of family have brought her to this new career of authorship. Susan's passion for life and new experiences led to the completion of this wonderful project. It is from that love and devotion that **WoW! What A Trip!** has come to be.

Acknowledgements

Sharing the joy of pregnancy with a child is a concept that needs to be illustrated in a way that allows the child to better understand the pregnancy. It took a long time and many interviews to find the illustrator. Susan Lavalley, artist, was just that person.

There were many others that helped along the way. My husband, Steven ignited the idea of the book, Shannon Tarrant (webmaster, editor, and everything), Tamara Tarrant and Makenna Egan, Erica (the inspiration for this book), Jordan (the reason for the book), Wendy and Bradley Adler, Tina Vogel, Larry Dickstein, Jim Lavalley, Rachael and Jessica Davis, Joseph Carolin, Pete Weaver, Leslie Weiss, Bijan Tabirzi, Carrie and Scott Sharapata, Moira and Jason Shiver, Theresa and Dennis Davis, Jill Gartman, Erin Morrell, Terry and Pauline Migrants, Jay and Barbara Gerber, Dr. Karen Hans, Vanessa and Chino, Chris Contreras, Eric Johnson, Dr. Joe Scarano, John T. Super, PH,D., ABPP, Kathy Thomas, Carmen Schettino, Barry Roth, and importantly, Mel Cohen (publishing consultant) all gave ideas, suggestions and invaluable inspiration.

Thankfully,
Susan M. Tarrant

Book Club Discussion Topics

What did you like best about this book?

How did your child/children react to this book?

What did you like least about the book?

Do you still have questions you would like the author to answer?

What other books have you read on the subject matter of this book?

Do like the book enough to recommend the book to others?

Are there other illustrations you would recommend?

Was the book appropriate for the 2-6 year old age group?

If not, at what age would you recommend?

Do the cover graphics and illustrations correctly

reflect the main topic of the book?

You can find the Book Club Discussion Topics and share your responses on our website:
www.wowwhatatripbook.com/bookclub

Congratulations!
WoW! What a Baby!

More books coming soon:

WoW! What a Trip!
Twins journey to meet their family

WoW! What a Trip!
The first year with my family

WoW! What a Trip!
Special Love for Special Needs

Visit the website: wowwhatatripbook.com to download the
full Parent Guide including conversation ideas and to share
your story of reading this book with your little ones.